Swans

and Other Poems

Mary Rae

ANCIENT CYPRESS PRESS
Fort Lauderdale

For Jeff

Ancient Cypress Press
Fort Lauderdale
Florida

ISBN: 978-0-9889648-0-8

Cover illustration: "Swans" by Mary Rae

Acknowledgments

These poems first appeared in the following journals as noted: "Seasons," in *The Raintown Review* (First Prize in the RR Poetry Contest, 2001); "The Golden Sky," "Reverie," "Lilacs in Boston," "Snow," "Reflection," "Circling Path," "Sometimes I Think," and "Year's End," in *Romantics Quarterly*; "Caruso," in *Hellas*; "For Keats," in *Piedmont Literary Review*; "Seer," in *Plains Poetry Journal*; "Palms," and "Tabula Rasa," in *The Neovictorian/ Cochlea*; "In The Night," in *Songs of Innocence*; "Tom," in *The Thomas Paine Society Newsletter* ; "I am Made For Clay," "I Don't Love You," and "Magic," in *Oregon Literary Review*; "Something Grows," in *Wyoming, The Hub of the Wheel*; "One Midnight," in *Carnelian*; "Swans," and "Lookout," in *The Eclectic Muse*; "Joint Custody," and "Daughter," in *The Lyric*; "Piano Composition," "That Evening," "Rooms," and "Your Melting Sky," in *The New Formalist*; "Letter From a Poet," in *The Hyper Texts*; "Giants," in *Sparrow*; "Creek," and "The Stars Tonight," in *Trinacria*; and "Sketch of a Man" in *Poetry Cornwall*.

Contents

Season	11
Circling Path	12
Expanding World	13
First Love	14
Gift	15
Reflection	16
Lilacs in Boston	17
Sometimes I Think	18
Swans	19
A Life of Many Houses	20
Seer	21
Sketch of a Man	22
Your Melting Sky	23
Almost Sufi	24
Friend	25
Life of Art	26
I Don't Love You	27
Guitar	28
Beside the Water	29
Galli-Curci	30
Piano Composition	31
Caruso	32
For Keats	33
Letter From a Poet	34
Giants	35
In the Everglades	36

Florida Storms   37

After the Hurricane   38

I Am Made for Clay   39

Palettes   40

In Virginia   41

Path   42

Visitor   43

Halfmoon   44

That Evening   45

Hills   46

Interlude   47

Reverie   48

The Golden Sky   50

In the Night   52

One Midnight   54

Black Magic   55

Pearl   56

K4EYG   57

For My Father   58

Creek   59

Tabula Rasa   60

Something Grows   61

My Daughter   62

Flying Kites   63

Stealing Magic   64

Her Kite   65

Blocks   66

Snow   67

Joint Custody   68

No Name   69

Lookout   70

Year's End   71

The Star's Tonight   72

Rooms   73

About Mary Rae   75

Swans

and Other Poems

Season

I

Youth and love unite beneath the power
of velvet skin and dark, half-sleeping eyes.
Spring seems to last forever to the flower
that feels the rush of chlorophyll's green rise.
Time is not—cannot be of the essence
when second hands are slow, standing still,
while all around the sun is streaming gold.
The thought of end, of beauty's obsolescence,
seems unreasonable and cannot hold
as long as love is dressed in daffodil.

II

Youth never sees itself or has a reason
to know that it has no infinity.
It turns, like Spring, a sweet, unknowing season,
never doubting its divinity.
But as in Fall trees look down on their leaves
that once had been too much a part to see,
powerless to reconstitute the whole;
so age sees fallen beauties and it grieves
the unclothing of the lonely soul
that, now in rags, goes begging tree to tree.

Circling Path

As I walk the circling path I see
trees sliding by, revealing bits of lake
between an arc of leaves and twigs that make
a frame of elegant geometry.
The turns come up at once, surprisingly,
as if a new uncoiling of a snake,
and though I am alone, that slow, dull ache
of shaded beauty keeps me company.
My loneliness seems small now, anyway,
a detail lost beneath the moving trees
whose shadows bury mine in somber blue;
and seeing myself lost among a spray
of ghostly branches floating by degrees
along the path, I turn and fall from view.

Expanding World

Some think the world gets smaller as we age
as family and friends desert the flock,
reminding us that soon a hollow knock
will summon jester, poet, fool and sage.
They'll march in silent prayer or silent rage,
but still in step with an unyielding clock
whose numbers fly with neither tick nor tock,
and mete out life in seconds, heartless gauge.
But since you've gone, it's turned out not to be
a shrinking world at all, but one that grows,
vast and multiplying in time's domain.
And though I search the crowds I cannot see
the face of one whose pallor says she knows
and cares that you were here and I remain.

First Love

The ancients took their treasures to the grave:
The golden cups, the fragrant wine for sips
when thirst should sear the afterworld. The ships
lay near in case a buried king might crave
a far off luxury. The ancients gave
such thought to dying, planning out their trips
into the future, and let go their grips
on those who lived, alone—to life, a slave.
And when your first love dies it's just the same.
They take with them the fragile cup of youth
and ships that floated on a velvet sea
for shores forever left without a name,
yet beautiful in possibility,
and gardens thick with love's unquestioned truth.

Gift

It sat among the other jewelry
as if it were an ordinary treasure,
but it remained while golden rings were lost.
In moves from place to place it anchored me,
a constant; in uncertain times, my measure,
my certainty that leaf would follow frost.

It was a locket given me by you
so long ago it seems another life,
before I'd thought in terms of man and wife,
before I even guessed time could imbue
an object with radiance; before I knew
I'd see you only one more time. No strife
can reach you now, but like a gentle knife
the locket carves one heart where once were two.

Reflection

Spirit houses slip into the lake,
almost black, and glittering, aflame
with quiet gold. Not sleeping, not awake,
figures float to fill a window frame,
dissolving as they rest, just dark again:
So little like their solid counterparts
whose fleshy arms crave both warmth and light
to make them capable of grace or sin,
to make them real, as if their touch, their sight
could make them masters of their liquid hearts.

Lilacs In Boston

There were lilacs all along the street;
people laughing, drunk with summer night.
The city seemed a globe of glass, complete
with moon that floated, starless, brilliant white.
The air stirred thick perfume into the mind,
turning it to love; then misery
of love that might not ever be returned.
Useless, then, a street sweet-lilac lined
for those who longed to kiss but could not see
the hand that stirred the love for which they yearned.

Sometimes I Think

Sometimes I think that, once upon a time,
there was a you meant only for a me,
that what I saw in you, essential, sublime,
was all there was or would ever be.
It wasn't hard to love your boyish charm
or the sadness of what your life had been,
but a soul, unfairly, can disarm
and blind true love to what else lies within.
If, perhaps, I had been a saint
my vision would have burned away the rust
that clung to spirit. But I was too faint
to love that long. The fairy tale is dust,
but like all tales began with something true:
I loved, a moment, something good in you.

Swans

Although I'll never again see the park
where we were married in a misting rain,
silvered into spirits, framed by bark,
black and wet, or the lake, domain
of swans slipping silently around
in circles, as if, in pairs, to celebrate
the rings we accepted without a sound,
innocent, not guessing our black fate;
although I won't return, I hope it stays
just as it was, September twenty-four,
a land of fairy dreams and golden days;
and if they come (who love forevermore),
I hope they do as the white swans bid,
and not waste aching beauty like we did.

A Life of Many Houses

So many houses—How did they divide
into one house that floats almost on blue
beneath a sun hot enough to brew
thick swamps where dull green alligators slide
onto the shore? It seems I was a bride
in Northern climes. It seems there was a view,
a pond with willow trees, an avenue
with someone walking always at my side.

If I could count the houses in between
that autumn and this chronic yellow heat
I'd find there wasn't one where life was broken.
But, I know, in every one I'd meet
the coming Everglades, steamy and green,
the home where love, at last, could leave no token.

Seer

I dreamed you were a murderer
and all the summer air
could not unblacken what you were
or make the body fair;

for what you killed was love itself,
its light and aching breath,
and though its limbs with studied grace
still moved, the dance was death.

Sketch of a Man

His eyes were black and burnt in sand,
his smile was shy, almost forlorn,
a prince left in an uncouth land,
he spoke with silky darkness shorn
from lengths of shoreline near his home
beneath white stars. His love was calm
and settled like a crown of foam
on one whose voice was his sweet psalm.
He loved her, but his arms would not
extend where his veiled iris drew
with small black threads a net that caught
soft light alone. He was, it's true,
accustomed to long waits, a man
who ached for evenings far and dim
when time would spread its paper fan
and send love's breath, at last, to him.

Your Melting Sky

I've saved the sound your shoes made as you walked
and kept the searing brilliance of your eyes,
and snow that warmed to water as you talked
dressing leathered death in spring's disguise.

That light embrace we thought would come again—
the one we cast away—I gathered up
and kept like new these thirty years for when
the water would spill back into the cup.

I've heard some noise of death, yes, of demise,
and listened to their tributes' rustling leaves,
and now a me that shadows me and cries
says love is measured only as it grieves;

but she says black and white, we live or die,
and doesn't know how much I've saved of you,
and while I stand beneath your melting sky
she searches for the man that she once knew.

Almost Sufi

Twirling in white
your robes aflame
you might have found
a different name.

How blue the light
the sea, so tame
with noiseless sound
that heavens claim.

You were in sight
but never came.
The dream unwound.
All was the same.

Friend

(for Kevin Roberts)

I knew your lines, so clean and made of light
that played against the somber songs you sang,
as faintly, far away, soft bell-tones rang
tolling twilight deep into your night.
You draped the hour of midnight over mirth
and darkened glittering joy with brevity.
I read of love that wasn't, but could be,
and love that never would be on this earth.
Your work was shimmering—was like a pool
on which your image wavered, not quite real,
but full of stars and moon to light the way.
You live still for the world, reflected jewel,
but I have lost the friend in you and feel
the loneliness of each unwritten day.

Life of Art

This sudden desire for beauty—
it's a dead giveaway.
The little lines around her mouth
the hair becoming grey.

Loveliness is passing
but she knows her life's a day.
And so she writes although in dreams
she'd rather be than say.

I Don't Love You

I don't love you, but I love a thought
that wears your face and body for a while
and lets me settle all my living, not
on you, but on something with your smile.

The dream of love, its ache and its embrace
are brief enough, but once again may live.
Perhaps a change of name or just of face
is all that love requires life to give.

Still, blackest nights of longing may succumb
to love made real, if only for a day,
and the heart, awake, no longer numb,
will let itself by flesh be rushed away,

and, in truth, I could love only you,
if you could see the thought that was just me.
But no. I see you dreaming, looking through
my eyes to what you think I'll never be.

Guitar

He played guitar for me that summer night
when archers made of stars drew back their bows
as if in ready for a spray of crows
that might be tossed by gods into their sight.
The pressure of his fingers was so slight
that soft harmonics out of silence rose
and found in air a moment of repose
decaying into thoughts of lost delight.
His songs were incantations made of air
breathed by an ancient sailor to align
his soul with stars to lead where he was bound.
He played guitar, but no immortal prayer
could reach the stars in shallow water drowned,
or lead where I was his, and he was mine.

Beside The Water

I kneel beside the water's trembling shore,
watching gold that pools and dissipates,
and feel less of the ground, the grass; and more
of water-life, of light. The sense sedates
my thinking self, my breath, my heaviness,
and leaves the faintest trace of life behind,
just a drop of light on spreading calm,
too small to feel, to hold, to curse or bless,
diluted further still in cooling balm;
and still I see you, though my soul is blind.

Galli-Curci (1889-1963)

Your voice was delicate beyond compare.
Amelita, were you lovely, too?
You must have let the rain run down your hair
to water earth with music as you do.
Did you feel the sunlight on your skin
and seek the solitude of wooded shade?
I've heard it in your voice once and again,
and even understand why you made
the "sweet" in "Home, Sweet Home," so very bright.
It was the nature of your smiling throat
and the way your eyes would fill with light.
Amelita, is life just a boat
that lets you steer through waves of deepening blue,
then sings through seas forever without you?

Piano Composition

There's D, F sharp and A, then D once more
all in the right, the left hand lingering
on two low notes that rumble as they sing
like a quiet storm. The field-like score
exists in seed in measures one through four
that know the moment when the chord will ring
and sympathetically vibrate each string
until sound fades—a slowly closing door.
Beginnings hold the end. An understanding
between composer and idea dictates
that one is slave until the piece is done.
A finished score is simply the unhanding
of what was always there—not work of fates—
but music whole the moment it's begun.

Caruso

I've heard it said your voice was great because
it's rare for notes so sweet to have an edge,
and that listening to your high notes was
like the thrill of standing on a ledge
where one false step would mean a spiral fall
past blurring windows lit to catch the eyes,
past fragrant trees whose branches seemed to call,
past the garden wall in slow surprise,
where time would deepen and grow wide,
past crocuses whose tender shoots would brush
against red cheeks, before the final slide
to earth: And as if that weren't enough,
no one listening could ever know
if you were holding on, or letting go.

For Keats

For you, who cannot tell the length of day
from a century, or even guess
from your hidden bower of quiet clay
if there are stars, or just black nothingness
where you once gauged your breath above the elms:
Although you left with many things unsaid,
heard now only in unknowing realms,
you, though you can't know it, are not dead
and have a life beyond your wildest dreams.
A waking dream: you kiss your love again
and lay your head against her skin like cream.
But, too late to make your love a friend—
your kind of dreaming never works that way.
It only thinks—as sun thinks up the day.

Letter From A Poet
(for Richard Moore)

The letter came adorned with just one stamp
with cancellation showing where the thought
of you first lit his mind and made him plot
his course. He drew some paper near a lamp
and grasped the pen that, in his steady hand,
could not be anything but orderly.
He could have sent an email off for free,
but felt, perhaps, what few would understand,
that there was life in paper and a pen;
not DNA, but bounties of intent.
And when he wrote of Catallus or Swift,
his ink would pool in seas beyond your ken,
and islands where he cut his mind adrift
would float across an age—the letter sent.

Giants

It is, some say, a wasteful shame to live
among the giants, dead as they are tall,
to pour bright dreams into a silver sieve
and watch them turn to powder as they fall.
How tiring to always think of up,
and strain to suck a thin and deadly air.
How sad, inviting Mr. Keats to sup,
and have him act as if you were not there.
Still, colossal minds will not erase,
their wakeful eyes tracing graceful lines
of jeweled planets spun in endless space
according to inevitable design.

In The Everglades

In the Everglades another fire
set off by lightning forms a twisting plume
of umber and burnt orange. Familiar gloom
drapes our spirit in dull black attire.
It's hard to dream, to hope and to aspire
to think of love, of lilac trees in bloom,
to sweep away throat-burning sense of doom
and shake the image of a funeral pyre.
We live too close to nature, some would say,
encroaching upon the wetlands, and deserve
whatever misfortune falls at whatever price.
But maybe we're just intruders anyway,
like nature's prey, we run, zigzag and swerve,
not quite at home in any paradise.

Florida Storms

In the tropics storms can be severe
and residents are watchers of the skies.
They know that blue euphoria belies
a gathering high in the atmosphere
that suddenly may break. To vanquish fear
alarms for lightning in the parks advise
all children to escape. A mom relies
on shrieking sirens to preserve what's dear.
Once safe inside she opens all the shades
and counts the bouncing hail, but lightning flashes,
and puts an end to electricity.
Now in the dark, her courage quickly fades
and out come candles as the thunder crashes,
small light against her frail mortality.

After the Hurricane

Even on the edge, it was despair,
although unharmed, untouched by deadly wind.
Spirit, like the palms, can't always bend,
and others' grief can be much grief to bear:
The buildings all undone, beyond repair;
unearthed oaks lying end to end;
the children who could never understand;
the thieves who plundered pain and could not care.
How dizzying the stench of rotting wood!
How wrenching all attempts to lend a hand!
But most unkind: the beauty of the sky,
full of gliding birds as if one could
lounge a thoughtless afternoon on sand
and let the ocean tell its calming lie.

I Am Made for Clay

The fall cannot be far, yet here I sit
amid the palms and birds of paradise
where parakeets of lime and yellow flit
through melon skies, where sapphire waves entice
young lovers from their homes, so far away;
and even storms with names cannot deter
their quest for sun so white it stings the eyes;
their ache for sand. But I am made for clay
that chills the heart along with oak and fir,
and gives it rest with every leaf that dies.

Palettes

Vandyke Brown, Raw Umber, Cassel Earth,
Golden Ochre, Naples Yellow Pale:
Northern colors, not of joy or mirth
but of restraint, born of winter's gale.
Somber colors bring back chilling years
in the North, grey and ill at ease.
I sketch a small dark room with small dark fears
far from my beloved dogwood trees.
Scrape the palette. Rub with turpentine.
Begin with Emerald green and Cobalt Blue.
For flowers add a touch of Red Carmine,
then paint the tropics, lovely, but too new.
But blend the palettes—tempered brilliance spills:
Virginia skies, forests, fields and hills.

In Virginia

The snow was like the snow of any year,
not softer on the tops of sable trees;
there was nothing in the slow degrees
of rising white to tell that you'd be near.

Nothing in the ice, though light and clear
and weighing branches down, had more to please,
to make my thoughts more love, more breath, more ease;
but still, you stood in silence with me here.

I didn't have to think, to conjure you,
to wish you with a wand of sparkling sleet:
You simply came, standing where I stood.

We watched as day was lost in evening's blue,
and when the moon rose making earth complete
you faded in the black, sweet-smelling wood.

Path

The path down to the woods is rough and steep
and framed by branches in whose lime-green glow
birds congregate and some sweet sabbath keep
and speak in tongues while humans pass below.
Now comes the creek, at last, the long descent
rewarded with a rushing melody,
with flies and frogs completing summer's choir.
A footstep breaks a branch—but sound's well spent,
sending squirrels in circles up a tree
that pierces heaven like some ancient spire.

Visitor

A little dove came to stay a while
and found our porch most accommodating.
The cushioned chair, it seemed, was just his style,
and there he sat, a prince of birds in waiting.
But if he hoped for health or cooler air
or just for a romantic interlude,
his eyes betrayed no joy and no despair,
nothing but unmoving solitude.
He may have thought of us—we'll never know—
but, for a moment, sat on the divide
of flying things and all the world below,
while we watched in silence, open-eyed,
wondering if he'd carry what he knew
of life below, of us, into the blue.

Halfmoon

The dog lies near, a halfmoon curve of black,
and waits. It looks like sleep, but stillness lies,
and ears are pricked for sound, and slivered eyes
say any moment he might join the pack,
might hear a far off howl and answer back,
then listen for another until the cries
of wolves emerge from beasts in dog disguise,
laying sound on sound for ears to track.
But he will never see the pack he knows,
and he will tire, as we all do, and sleep,
and let his world of fearsome grandeur fade.
Then I will watch, imagining he goes
with dogs in dreams, until my own dreams keep
a vigil over unseen worlds I've made.

That Evening

There must have been a million stars but I
take that on faith, and have no memory
of looking up at all. A quiet sea
of phosphorescence was a lullaby
to all my senses, and I did not reply
to words that fell like far off bells, while he
stood near his cabin door. I couldn't see,
but felt him as one feels a firefly
is circling near although its light is gone.
It was his world, but wasn't mine for keeping,
and so I left as if I'd come again.
But, like an antique lamp that we turn on
to light our thoughts although we'll soon be sleeping,
that evening flickers now as it did then.

Hills

The hills descend and rise till trees emerge
and cradle trembling fields in golden arms.
So vast the eyes above, so great the urge
to breathe aloud, setting off alarms
of birds into the blue. The earth seems still,
and yet its face must color dark and change.
But, a field like this, this drop, this hill,
cannot be shifted, cannot become strange
to one who's ever knelt into the grass
and shared the greening air of bending flowers.
It will remain, its likeness never pass,
and in each blade will live the drowsy hours
which, like loving parents, shall appear
to call out, "Sleep, my child, for we are near."

Interlude

For just a moment I could feel no breath
no sinking blood, no heat, no cold, no motion
as if the trees had parted leaving death
alone with life, each filled with still devotion.

There was no joy, no boredom, no regret,
no long ago, no now, no coming days,
no contemplation, hope or fear, and yet,
you burned like diamond sunlight through the haze.

And all I knew was just what I could feel,
a presence in the emptiness of being
becoming me, for just one moment—real,
blind to life, but in the darkness, seeing.

Reverie

I walked beside the ocean in a dream
and watched it swell and shrink and part and merge,
and slide from oxide green to yellow-grey,
opaque, then shot with light where golden fish
were caught a moment, in uncertainty
that reddened gold and bronzed their stippled orange
before they blackened back to sea again,
leaving me to wonder what I'd seen,
or if I'd seen at all. A hundred clouds
in shifting shapes, white with silver edges,
turning, rolling into clay-like fields
of umber, almost black, and burnt sienna,
crossed high above the water with such speed
I could imagine purpose to their flight.
But purpose, plans, and hope were human things,
and I, beside the water, by myself,
could think of nothing future, nothing past,
but only light that scattered on the sand,
so filled with salt, with remnants of what was—
a brick-red crab, an empty pink-lined shell,
an oyster left without the glistening pearl
that made us think it beautiful and worth
our measured human touch. The tender spray
of so much life against my face grew warm,
so like a kiss, so like the first embrace,
the very first when love was only joy
of rising froth and upward-spilling light;
a light connecting life to other life
to let the spirit wake and know itself,
and let it play among all living things,
to move and grow and shift and touch the world,
changing it with subtle water motion
that pulled on every thought; to let it feel

the rush of pain and pleasure's slow sweet rise,
the shock of brilliant reds, the strange pefumes,
that lured the mind into silent woods
where every breath was felt, and every pulse
of blood was known within the heart itself;
to let it find, in the changing shape
of living, its own perfect changelessness;
to let it live, and let it then sink back
into the shining black of hidden depths
where spirits moved like unseeing fish,
not knowing of their selves, not of the sea,
sealed in darkness, never knowing light,
or life itself. I felt the water rise,
as if to wash humanity away
with blinding foam, too much to feel and see—
and so I woke.
              The dream was not of you.
I never thought of you or longed at all
to see your figure standing, looking out,
gold against the green of churning waves.
The dream was not of you, but when I woke
your face appeared and filled the aching hollow
the sea had carved so deep into my heart,
still red with life, before it ebbed away.

The Golden Sky

Stand by me now, and fall and kiss my feet
and let your linen touch the umber earth,
and I will lay my hand across your hair
with spice and fragrant almond oil made sweet,
and tears will pool beneath your burning prayer
reflecting back a sky of topaz mirth:

The golden sky, the sky you've longed to love,
to see each day upon awakening,
to light the sands, the rippling tops of trees,
to gild a leaf or bronze an amber dove
or lighten yellow of the circling bees
that rise then disappear in olive green.

And there below, the path where, through the hills,
you would walk among the human throng
is brightening. You ache to touch one hand,
to breathe one breath, to stand among the wills
of a thousand minds that can command
their lips to kiss, or part in evensong.

You dream of waking on a straw-filled bed
to feel your neck grown stiff and full of pain,
to know the weight of throbbing legs and hips.
You long for wine and steaming loaves of bread,
to taste the blood-red liquid on your lips
that, from long savoring, would bear its stain,

the red of life, of hearts that rise and sink,
the mark of living in this world below.
But, see your lips, look in your pool of tears:
your mouth is clean, there is no wine to drink,
and as you reach for life it disappears.
What you knew once, you never more shall know.

But stay, and wash my feet and understand
that I, who called in dark to have you near,
and thought this living too much life to bear,
will hold you close, lend you my eye, my hand;
and let you breathe the cool and coursing air
and watch as mountain waters reappear

in morning gold. And you shall have your wine,
and use my lips as if they were your own,
and fall in happiness to budding earth.
And tears that were your tears shall now be mine,
and I will save one golden leaf alone
to show you what a crown of thorns is worth.

In The Night

In the night
the secret night
the night of dark perfuming

blossoms wait
and waters wait
for the day's unblooming.

Turning back
ticking back
into a timeless time:

No clock can set
no hand can set
the motionless sublime.

No subtle thought
no searching thought
can lift the lightest veils

or guess the form
the endless form
that formlessness entails.

Unthinking life
unbreathing life
is all there is to know

in the night
the sightless night
all lovely light entombing;

in the night
the secret night
the night of dark perfuming.

One Midnight

I left my house because you were not there
and every light was burning to bring back
your face, so calm, your dark and gleaming hair,
but when I turned to see you, all was black.

I left to seek you in the midnight sky
that knew your beauties, counting star by star.
I could not breathe for feeling you close by,
but turned to see the sky grown cold and far.

The fields brushed evening's wet against my feet
and distant mountains held still pools of light.
I heard you call. The air grew thick and sweet.
I wandered after you into the night.

But only birds called back from bending trees
that blended into dawn's first golden red.
The grass was soft. I rested on my knees
beside a stream, and knew that I was dead.

And in my loneliness I cupped my hand
to drink of earth's cool water one last time.
But as I bent to drink the air was fanned
with spice which made the water's taste sublime.

I looked into the water's stirring face
and saw a light that changed what I had been,
leaving you forever in my place,
and giving me, with love, my life again.

Black Magic

There is black magic in a photograph.
We stare through smoke and think a contact made.
So strong the sense of flesh and life displayed
we watch a smile condensing from a laugh.
An instant so completely fresh and sealed
is like a pause between beats of a heart—
for flowing blood, a solid, resting form.
And like a message rolled across a field
of sudden void just before a storm,
it proves life's quiet holds its greatest art.

Pearl

I

I never met you, but I know you well.
Your smile, your chin, your hair, your dark brown eyes
are features that I wear and plagiarize
as if I'd crawled into your empty shell.
Such resemblance, Grandmother, is strange,
and forces me to delve into our genes
and wonder if the strands that made us so
would have made us likely to exchange
thoughts on Wordsworth, Titian, and Rousseau,
and on the line dividing blues and greens.

II

I heard you liked to sing, and so do I,
but was there matching resonance and tone?
And did you like to spend long hours alone
in heavy silence? I'll never verify
the similarities that I infer,
and feel deprived that you died of the flu
so very young, at only twenty-six,
leaving memories all in a blur,
too jumbled for your little boy to fix
into a coherent, breathing you.

K4EYG

Kilo four echo yankee gulf,
a call that any Ham would understand
as K4EYG, the K for land
west of the Mississippi. Off the cuff
conversations sent by radio waves
formed the background of a child's years,
with quiet static, music without staves.
Who would not replay the magic hour
when family was written, signed and sealed,
all there ever was, would ever be?
Time is slowing, thickened and congealed,
glistening beneath an endless shower
of voices calling: K4EYG.

For My Father

I

The pipers led us down the summer hill
into a thick blue shade. The shifting air
supplied a rushing quiet to repair
the rest between the notes. He played until
another spoke, impossible to hear
over admonitions that arose
silently, to do what must be done.
In life—a father, husband, engineer,
a gardener and even once, a son;
In death—a door that no one wants to close.

II

A sound draws up our loving disbelief
and gathers it along a black despair:
To hear his voice, thinking he is there,
knowing all the while, is sinking grief.
We wouldn't wish him back into his pain
and see him in the world that he was in
or watch him take that road of sad decline.
But if we chose one moment to regain,
we'd stand, his seven children, in a line,
and watch him tend his roses once again.

Creek

It wasn't easy walking to the creek.
The path was steep and strewn with leaf and stone.
The little russian blue, so grey and sleek,
Would never let them hazard it alone,
and walked two steps ahead along the path
while they delighted in their gleaming guide
who'd step into the creek for half a bath
and leap, still sparkling, to the other side.

The woman hasn't seen the creek in years.
The cat died long ago, then it was he
who left this life for one that she can't know.
She takes the walk in dreams—The cat appears,
but what she feels is what she cannot see:
The arm that will not let her fall below.

Tabula Rasa

What is this sad and alien world
into which they've come,
with field and sky unclean, and darkened sea?

With a flag of plague unfurled
and slowly beating drum,
the shrinking earth disputes eternity.

Yet, like flowers, children grow
beneath the finite shade,
and every leaf they touch they consecrate.

They rise and stretch their arms to show
how beautifully they're made,
and turn the world into a virgin slate.

Something Grows

My little boys are digging in the dirt.
This is their garden fashioned with a will
that's never heard of seeds and never heard
of fertilize, or weed, or roto-till.
And so they raise bright apples next to flowers
that must spring up from new earth-covered grass,
and all they need is sunshine and brief showers:
This is how a garden comes to pass.
Invisible does not mean, "is not real,"
to little boys who taste in earth itself
the possibility of fruit and deal
with living things like new toys on a shelf.
And though their little harvest never shows,
they know that somehow, somewhere, something grows.

My Daughter

My daughter sits, all beauty, on the horse
and with her legs invites a civil trot.
Her chin is up, her eyes survey the course
with queenly calm. Now and then a thought
of heels down or steady hands intrudes,
reminding her that she has much to learn,
is just beginning, but her joy precludes
doubting and impatience. The horse will turn
with her urging. Now a figure eight,
keeping close inside along the rail.
She and the horse must negotiate
the give and take, so neither will prevail
but both, in time, will breathe a single air
and think as one—the two become a pair.

Flying Kites

Looking at the two of you across
the waterway, I felt I had become
an awkward lighthouse waiting for a lost
ship's return. A father and a son
suddenly so small against the sand,
suddenly you both so unlike me.
The kite rose up and took the air, an ensign
above the ship that invisibly
swept you from my light, into an ocean
and unknown shores. The two of you were caught
for just one breath beneath the spiraling wind.
And I could read the flag's bright letters: Not
"Father and Son," what you had always been,
but what I could not touch—simply : "Men."

Stealing Magic

All trees are magic. They appear
as giants to a child in flight,
looming promises of fear:
One part spirit; one part night.
No tree has form, solidity,
but, long deserted, may arise
and, as if to prove it real,
we measure, weigh and memorize,
and thinking we have caught a tree,
all its potent magic steal.

Her Kite

The grass looks yellow green and trees beyond
are greenish grey and fade into cold white
of sky whose only traveler is a kite
kept aloft invisibly. What bond
of child with sky says sky will not abscond
with paper instruments of child delight
with just a wooden cross to shape its flight
and string as faithful as a shepherd's wand?
The kite is known—the child is just a guess.
We cannot see, but trust she is at play
and know, with her, that paper things can fly.
And when the wind picks up, her happiness
is in our hands and we must turn away
to keep her kite forever in the sky.

Blocks

You build with blocks, and thoroughfares
have elegant parquet, the portals
rise up to rest smooth walls and stairs.
Of gods' revenge on lovely mortals
in lands of white built on an isle
of dreams, starward from sea below,
you can't have heard in your short time;
and yet, your little people climb
up to the top in single file
and cry out: No! No! No!

Snow

Snow is falling, brilliant white from grey,
soft and silent like a magic rain
of fairy dust waved by a candy cane,
while children listen for a phantom sleigh.
What of the jingling bells? The overlay
of crunching snow and carolers' refrain
fall at once into the child's domain
of Happiness, of Joy, of Holiday.
You cannot tell a child to not believe
what her bright imagination knows,
and what her eyes and ears tell her is true.
And, in years to come, on Christmas Eve,
she'll look back to when her joy was new,
and wish, once more, for enchanted snows.

Joint Custody

They've decided to divide the child.
Three days with one, and four days with the other.
They say her feelings will, at most, be mild
discomfort; that her father and her mother
will share her joys this way, and keep her whole;
a child of parents, not just one, but two,
leaving both their marks of love. Their goal
is just her happiness, and all they do
is for her good, not theirs. A little girl
cannot yet know where her best interest lies,
and so must trust to others. But the pearl
of little teeth won't show, and her blue eyes
are darkening, as if she held inside
a little something no one can divide.

No Name

When all the nights you stayed awake to bathe
their sweating brows, and all the lightless days
of ironing and sweeping and dull aches
for ancient things and poetry; when the way
you brought out burning stars as you sang
your little ones to sleep; when how you stayed
beside them just to taste the air that they'd
distilled; when all of this has finally changed
the way the birches bend, has changed the shape
of the hills where thin grey horses chase
your little foxes; when the creek is stained
a different brown, and every little place
you ever walked reflects your changing face,
then—you will know that no such thing as fame
could touch the world as you have, with no name.

Lookout

The house was like a lookout on the hill
set to survey the woods that spread below
and there, beyond, a field that held a school,
a citadel with further woods that ran
into the slate blue mountains. It seemed right
that earth should offer up its graceful trees,
its glittering fields for people who would gaze
like royalty in awe of their domain,
a land, made theirs, of bright, unchanging joy.
But as the seasons drew the years around,
wave after wave and blurring end to end;
as children came and went and hair grew grey,
the woods drew closer, circling the house,
obliterating golden swathes of field
until the stately school was cut from view
and hopes of glimpsing it again were lost.

It took a lifetime to observe the change
and think that, finally, nature would reclaim
each stalwart fort, returning brick to clay.
It took that long to lay aside the crown,
to feel the weight of brimming watering can
and spade and rake; to wear a gardener's look
of tenderness for newly planted trees
that would outlive the hands that patted them
into the ground a hundred years or more.
It took that long, but at the end of day
the people could look out across the woods,
grown dense and closer still, and see the life
of every tree that ever grew on earth
and understand, at last, a garden's joy.

Year's End

I come again to see the winter new,
not grey and spare, but delicate and light,
with limbs so deftly painted, taking flight
above mute green into an ancient blue.
No colors pure, but mixed with earthly hue,
the scene falls softly like a veiling night,
a respite from too green, too blue, too bright,
and sun whose glare renders sight untrue.
I see the land as once it was to me:
neither bleak nor brilliant, white nor black;
but beautiful, well-tempered, full and sweet.
Winter draws up life's entirety
into a year where earth's life is complete,
and all the world, like me, is looking back.

The Stars Tonight

The stars tonight are soft and barely lit
like rose-cut diamonds spread in giant hands
that stretch from present earth to older lands
to show what rare, faint light the stones emit.
You'd think there were too many stars to fit
my human hands, but memory that spans
the decades opens like enormous fans,
ensuring that their flame will never quit.
The stars tonight could never be mistaken
for any but the stars that, long years past,
rotated with the night above our faces.
Little did we think we would awaken
to find the stars had stolen our embraces,
and saved the light of love that wouldn't last.

Rooms

Every room I've ever seen is here.
This studio with six-foot squares of light
gives way as I pass through. Another room,
familiar in the way it empties me
of hope, of sorrow, joy and fear, of life,
wears me, for a moment, like a dream
it had when it first rose from nails and wood
in frozen climes, then it releases me
into the sun again. How many other
rooms took hold I'll never know for sure,
but they together make me doubt the truth
of happiness I held one hour ago,
of dread I nurtured for what dark could come.
Now, paper, pen and books and music scores,
place-holders for a life, lie strewn about
the rooms that shift from snow to glaring sun.

About Mary Rae

Mary Rae's poetry has been published in many journals over the years. For several years, she was editor-in-chief of *Romantics Quarterly*, having taken over for poet Kevin N. Roberts. Holding a degree in Spanish Language and Literature from Boston University, Mary is also a translator whose book, *St. John of the Cross:Selected Poems*, was originally published by Longwood Academic, and is now available in a revised, illustrated version. Mary Rae is also an artist and illustrator, and a composer of contemporary classical music. Examples of her music may be found on her site, www.maryraemusic.com. A native of Virginia, Mary has lived for many years in South Florida.